"To walk in nature is to witness a thousand miracles."

– Mary Davis

TRAIL NAME

RATE/EXPERIENCE

DATE

LOCATION

COMPANIONS

WEATHER CONDITION

☐ ☐ ☐ ☐ ☐

START TIME

END TIME

DURATION

DISTANCE

ALTITUDE

TERRAIN LEVEL

easy ☐ ☐ ☐ ☐ ☐ hard

GEAR & EQUIPMENT

TRAIL TYPE

Out & back ☐ Loop ☐

One way ☐ Other ☐

MILESTONES

HIGHLIGHTS

TO DO NEXT TIME

MY HIKING NOTES

TRAIL NAME

RATE/EXPERIENCE

DATE

LOCATION

COMPANIONS

WEATHER CONDITION

☐ ☐ ☐ ☐ ☐

TERRAIN LEVEL

easy ☐ ☐ ☐ ☐ ☐ hard

TRAIL TYPE

Out & back ☐ Loop ☐

One way ☐ Other ☐

START TIME

END TIME

DURATION

DISTANCE

ALTITUDE

GEAR & EQUIPMENT

MILESTONES

HIGHLIGHTS

TO DO NEXT TIME

MY HIKING NOTES

TRAIL NAME

RATE/EXPERIENCE

DATE

LOCATION

COMPANIONS

WEATHER CONDITION

TERRAIN LEVEL

easy hard

TRAIL TYPE

Out & back

Loop

One way

Other

START TIME

END TIME

DURATION

DISTANCE

ALTITUDE

GEAR & EQUIPMENT

MILESTONES

HIGHLIGHTS

TO DO NEXT TIME

MY HIKING NOTES

TRAIL NAME

RATE/EXPERIENCE

DATE

LOCATION

COMPANIONS

WEATHER CONDITION

TERRAIN LEVEL

easy hard

TRAIL TYPE

Out & back

Loop

One way

Other

MILESTONES

START TIME

END TIME

DURATION

DISTANCE

ALTITUDE

GEAR & EQUIPMENT

HIGHLIGHTS

TO DO NEXT TIME

MY HIKING NOTES

TRAIL NAME

RATE/EXPERIENCE

DATE

LOCATION

COMPANIONS

WEATHER CONDITION

TERRAIN LEVEL

easy ☐ ☐ ☐ ☐ ☐ hard

TRAIL TYPE

Out & back ☐ Loop ☐

One way ☐ Other ☐

START TIME

END TIME

DURATION

DISTANCE

ALTITUDE

GEAR & EQUIPMENT

MILESTONES

HIGHLIGHTS

TO DO NEXT TIME

MY HIKING NOTES

TRAIL NAME

RATE/EXPERIENCE

DATE

LOCATION

COMPANIONS

WEATHER CONDITION

TERRAIN LEVEL

easy ☐ ☐ ☐ ☐ ☐ hard

TRAIL TYPE

Out & back ☐ Loop ☐

One way ☐ Other ☐

MILESTONES

START TIME

END TIME

DURATION

DISTANCE

ALTITUDE

GEAR & EQUIPMENT

HIGHLIGHTS

TO DO NEXT TIME

MY HIKING NOTES

TRAIL NAME ☆☆☆☆☆

RATE/EXPERIENCE

DATE

LOCATION

COMPANIONS

WEATHER CONDITION

☐ ☐ ☐ ☐ ☐

TERRAIN LEVEL

easy ☐ ☐ ☐ ☐ ☐ hard

TRAIL TYPE

Out & back ☐ Loop ☐

One way ☐ Other ☐

MILESTONES

START TIME

END TIME

DURATION

DISTANCE

ALTITUDE

GEAR & EQUIPMENT

HIGHLIGHTS

TO DO NEXT TIME

MY HIKING NOTES

TRAIL NAME

RATE/EXPERIENCE

DATE

LOCATION

COMPANIONS

WEATHER CONDITION

☐ ☐ ☐ ☐ ☐

TERRAIN LEVEL

easy ☐ ☐ ☐ ☐ ☐ hard

TRAIL TYPE

Out & back ☐ Loop ☐

One way ☐ Other ☐

MILESTONES

START TIME

END TIME

DURATION

DISTANCE

ALTITUDE

GEAR & EQUIPMENT

HIGHLIGHTS

TO DO NEXT TIME

MY HIKING NOTES

TRAIL NAME

RATE/EXPERIENCE

DATE

LOCATION

COMPANIONS

WEATHER CONDITION

START TIME

END TIME

DURATION

DISTANCE

ALTITUDE

TERRAIN LEVEL

easy ☐ ☐ ☐ ☐ ☐ hard

GEAR & EQUIPMENT

TRAIL TYPE

Out & back ☐ Loop ☐

One way ☐ Other ☐

MILESTONES

HIGHLIGHTS

TO DO NEXT TIME

MY HIKING NOTES

TRAIL NAME

RATE/EXPERIENCE

DATE

LOCATION

COMPANIONS

WEATHER CONDITION

TERRAIN LEVEL

easy ☐ ☐ ☐ ☐ ☐ hard

TRAIL TYPE

Out & back ☐ Loop ☐

One way ☐ Other ☐

START TIME

END TIME

DURATION

DISTANCE

ALTITUDE

GEAR & EQUIPMENT

MILESTONES

HIGHLIGHTS

TO DO NEXT TIME

MY HIKING NOTES

TRAIL NAME

RATE/EXPERIENCE

DATE

LOCATION

COMPANIONS

WEATHER CONDITION

TERRAIN LEVEL

easy hard

TRAIL TYPE

Out & back

Loop

One way

Other

START TIME

END TIME

DURATION

DISTANCE

ALTITUDE

GEAR & EQUIPMENT

MILESTONES

HIGHLIGHTS

TO DO NEXT TIME

MY HIKING NOTES

TRAIL NAME

RATE/EXPERIENCE

DATE

LOCATION

COMPANIONS

WEATHER CONDITION

START TIME

END TIME

DURATION

DISTANCE

ALTITUDE

TERRAIN LEVEL

easy ☐ ☐ ☐ ☐ ☐ hard

GEAR & EQUIPMENT

TRAIL TYPE

Out & back ☐ Loop ☐

One way ☐ Other ☐

MILESTONES

HIGHLIGHTS

TO DO NEXT TIME

MY HIKING NOTES

TRAIL NAME

RATE/EXPERIENCE

DATE

LOCATION

COMPANIONS

WEATHER CONDITION

☐ ☐ ☐ ☐ ☐

TERRAIN LEVEL

easy ☐ ☐ ☐ ☐ ☐ hard

TRAIL TYPE

Out & back ☐ Loop ☐

One way ☐ Other ☐

START TIME

END TIME

DURATION

DISTANCE

ALTITUDE

GEAR & EQUIPMENT

MILESTONES

HIGHLIGHTS

TO DO NEXT TIME

MY HIKING NOTES

TRAIL NAME

RATE/EXPERIENCE

DATE

LOCATION

COMPANIONS

WEATHER CONDITION

TERRAIN LEVEL

easy ☐ ☐ ☐ ☐ ☐ hard

TRAIL TYPE

Out & back ☐ Loop ☐

One way ☐ Other ☐

MILESTONES

START TIME

END TIME

DURATION

DISTANCE

ALTITUDE

GEAR & EQUIPMENT

HIGHLIGHTS

TO DO NEXT TIME

MY HIKING NOTES

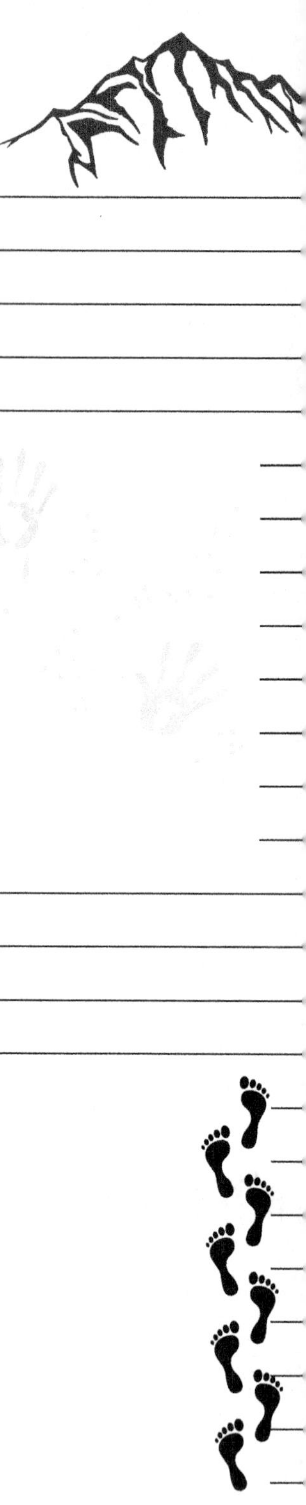

TRAIL NAME

RATE/EXPERIENCE

DATE

LOCATION

COMPANIONS

WEATHER CONDITION

START TIME

END TIME

DURATION

DISTANCE

ALTITUDE

TERRAIN LEVEL

easy ☐ ☐ ☐ ☐ ☐ hard

GEAR & EQUIPMENT

TRAIL TYPE

Out & back ☐ Loop ☐

One way ☐ Other ☐

MILESTONES

HIGHLIGHTS

TO DO NEXT TIME

MY HIKING NOTES

TRAIL NAME

RATE/EXPERIENCE

DATE

LOCATION

COMPANIONS

WEATHER CONDITION

TERRAIN LEVEL

easy ☐ ☐ ☐ ☐ ☐ hard

TRAIL TYPE

Out & back ☐ Loop ☐

One way ☐ Other ☐

START TIME

END TIME

DURATION

DISTANCE

ALTITUDE

GEAR & EQUIPMENT

MILESTONES

HIGHLIGHTS

TO DO NEXT TIME

MY HIKING NOTES

TRAIL NAME

RATE/EXPERIENCE

DATE

LOCATION

COMPANIONS

WEATHER CONDITION

☐ ☐ ☐ ☐ ☐

START TIME

END TIME

DURATION

DISTANCE

ALTITUDE

TERRAIN LEVEL

easy ☐ ☐ ☐ ☐ ☐ hard

GEAR & EQUIPMENT

TRAIL TYPE

Out & back ☐ Loop ☐

One way ☐ Other ☐

MILESTONES

HIGHLIGHTS

TO DO NEXT TIME

MY HIKING NOTES

TRAIL NAME

RATE/EXPERIENCE

DATE

LOCATION

COMPANIONS

WEATHER CONDITION

START TIME

END TIME

DURATION

DISTANCE

ALTITUDE

TERRAIN LEVEL

easy ☐ ☐ ☐ ☐ ☐ hard

GEAR & EQUIPMENT

TRAIL TYPE

Out & back ☐ Loop ☐

One way ☐ Other ☐

MILESTONES

HIGHLIGHTS

TO DO NEXT TIME

MY HIKING NOTES

TRAIL NAME

RATE/EXPERIENCE

DATE

LOCATION

COMPANIONS

WEATHER CONDITION

☐ ☐ ☐ ☐ ☐

START TIME

END TIME

DURATION

DISTANCE

ALTITUDE

TERRAIN LEVEL

easy ☐ ☐ ☐ ☐ ☐ hard

GEAR & EQUIPMENT

TRAIL TYPE

Out & back ☐ Loop ☐

One way ☐ Other ☐

MILESTONES

HIGHLIGHTS

TO DO NEXT TIME

MY HIKING NOTES

TRAIL NAME

RATE/EXPERIENCE

DATE

LOCATION

COMPANIONS

WEATHER CONDITION

☐ ☐ ☐ ☐ ☐

START TIME

END TIME

DURATION

DISTANCE

ALTITUDE

TERRAIN LEVEL

easy ☐ ☐ ☐ ☐ ☐ hard

GEAR & EQUIPMENT

TRAIL TYPE

Out & back ☐ Loop ☐

One way ☐ Other ☐

MILESTONES

HIGHLIGHTS

TO DO NEXT TIME

MY HIKING NOTES

TRAIL NAME

RATE/EXPERIENCE

DATE

LOCATION

COMPANIONS

WEATHER CONDITION

TERRAIN LEVEL

easy hard

TRAIL TYPE

Out & back

Loop

One way

Other

START TIME

END TIME

DURATION

DISTANCE

ALTITUDE

GEAR & EQUIPMENT

MILESTONES

HIGHLIGHTS

TO DO NEXT TIME

MY HIKING NOTES

TRAIL NAME

RATE/EXPERIENCE

DATE

LOCATION

COMPANIONS

WEATHER CONDITION

TERRAIN LEVEL

easy ☐ ☐ ☐ ☐ ☐ hard

TRAIL TYPE

Out & back ☐ Loop ☐

One way ☐ Other ☐

START TIME

END TIME

DURATION

DISTANCE

ALTITUDE

GEAR & EQUIPMENT

MILESTONES

HIGHLIGHTS

TO DO NEXT TIME

MY HIKING NOTES

TRAIL NAME

RATE/EXPERIENCE

DATE

LOCATION

COMPANIONS

WEATHER CONDITION

☐ ☐ ☐ ☐ ☐

TERRAIN LEVEL

easy ☐ ☐ ☐ ☐ ☐ hard

TRAIL TYPE

Out & back ☐ Loop ☐
One way ☐ Other ☐

MILESTONES

START TIME

END TIME

DURATION

DISTANCE

ALTITUDE

GEAR & EQUIPMENT

HIGHLIGHTS

TO DO NEXT TIME

MY HIKING NOTES

TRAIL NAME

RATE/EXPERIENCE

DATE

LOCATION

COMPANIONS

WEATHER CONDITION

TERRAIN LEVEL

easy ☐ ☐ ☐ ☐ ☐ hard

TRAIL TYPE

Out & back ☐ Loop ☐

One way ☐ Other ☐

START TIME

END TIME

DURATION

DISTANCE

ALTITUDE

GEAR & EQUIPMENT

MILESTONES

HIGHLIGHTS

TO DO NEXT TIME

MY HIKING NOTES

TRAIL NAME

RATE/EXPERIENCE

DATE

LOCATION

COMPANIONS

WEATHER CONDITION

☐ ☐ ☐ ☐ ☐

START TIME

END TIME

DURATION

DISTANCE

ALTITUDE

TERRAIN LEVEL

easy ☐ ☐ ☐ ☐ ☐ hard

GEAR & EQUIPMENT

TRAIL TYPE

Out & back ☐ Loop ☐

One way ☐ Other ☐

MILESTONES

HIGHLIGHTS

TO DO NEXT TIME

MY HIKING NOTES

TRAIL NAME

RATE/EXPERIENCE

DATE

LOCATION

COMPANIONS

WEATHER CONDITION

TERRAIN LEVEL

easy hard

TRAIL TYPE

Out & back
Loop
One way
Other

START TIME
END TIME
DURATION
DISTANCE
ALTITUDE

GEAR & EQUIPMENT

MILESTONES

HIGHLIGHTS

TO DO NEXT TIME

MY HIKING NOTES

TRAIL NAME

RATE/EXPERIENCE

DATE

LOCATION

COMPANIONS

WEATHER CONDITION

TERRAIN LEVEL

easy hard

TRAIL TYPE

Out & back

Loop

One way

Other

MILESTONES

START TIME

END TIME

DURATION

DISTANCE

ALTITUDE

GEAR & EQUIPMENT

HIGHLIGHTS

TO DO NEXT TIME

MY HIKING NOTES

TRAIL NAME

RATE/EXPERIENCE

DATE

LOCATION

COMPANIONS

WEATHER CONDITION

START TIME

END TIME

DURATION

DISTANCE

ALTITUDE

TERRAIN LEVEL

easy ☐ ☐ ☐ ☐ ☐ hard

GEAR & EQUIPMENT

TRAIL TYPE

Out & back ☐ Loop ☐

One way ☐ Other ☐

MILESTONES

HIGHLIGHTS

TO DO NEXT TIME

MY HIKING NOTES

TRAIL NAME

RATE/EXPERIENCE

DATE

LOCATION

COMPANIONS

WEATHER CONDITION

☐ ☐ ☐ ☐ ☐

TERRAIN LEVEL

easy ☐ ☐ ☐ ☐ ☐ hard

TRAIL TYPE

Out & back ☐ Loop ☐

One way ☐ Other ☐

START TIME

END TIME

DURATION

DISTANCE

ALTITUDE

GEAR & EQUIPMENT

MILESTONES

HIGHLIGHTS

TO DO NEXT TIME

MY HIKING NOTES

TRAIL NAME

RATE/EXPERIENCE

DATE

LOCATION

COMPANIONS

WEATHER CONDITION

☐ ☐ ☐ ☐ ☐

TERRAIN LEVEL

easy ☐ ☐ ☐ ☐ ☐ hard

TRAIL TYPE

Out & back ☐ Loop ☐

One way ☐ Other ☐

START TIME

END TIME

DURATION

DISTANCE

ALTITUDE

GEAR & EQUIPMENT

MILESTONES

HIGHLIGHTS

TO DO NEXT TIME

MY HIKING NOTES

TRAIL NAME

RATE/EXPERIENCE

DATE

LOCATION

COMPANIONS

WEATHER CONDITION

☐ ☐ ☐ ☐ ☐

TERRAIN LEVEL

easy ☐ ☐ ☐ ☐ ☐ hard

TRAIL TYPE

Out & back ☐ Loop ☐

One way ☐ Other ☐

START TIME

END TIME

DURATION

DISTANCE

ALTITUDE

GEAR & EQUIPMENT

MILESTONES

HIGHLIGHTS

TO DO NEXT TIME

MY HIKING NOTES

TRAIL NAME

RATE/EXPERIENCE

DATE

LOCATION

COMPANIONS

WEATHER CONDITION

☐ ☐ ☐ ☐ ☐

START TIME

END TIME

DURATION

DISTANCE

ALTITUDE

TERRAIN LEVEL

easy ☐ ☐ ☐ ☐ ☐ hard

GEAR & EQUIPMENT

TRAIL TYPE

Out & back ☐ Loop ☐

One way ☐ Other ☐

MILESTONES

HIGHLIGHTS

TO DO NEXT TIME

MY HIKING NOTES

TRAIL NAME

RATE/EXPERIENCE

DATE

LOCATION

COMPANIONS

WEATHER CONDITION

START TIME

END TIME

DURATION

DISTANCE

ALTITUDE

TERRAIN LEVEL

easy ☐ ☐ ☐ ☐ ☐ hard

GEAR & EQUIPMENT

TRAIL TYPE

Out & back ☐ Loop ☐

One way ☐ Other ☐

MILESTONES

HIGHLIGHTS

TO DO NEXT TIME

MY HIKING NOTES

TRAIL NAME

RATE/EXPERIENCE

DATE

LOCATION

COMPANIONS

WEATHER CONDITION

TERRAIN LEVEL

easy ☐ ☐ ☐ ☐ ☐ hard

TRAIL TYPE

Out & back ☐ Loop ☐

One way ☐ Other ☐

START TIME

END TIME

DURATION

DISTANCE

ALTITUDE

GEAR & EQUIPMENT

MILESTONES

HIGHLIGHTS

TO DO NEXT TIME

MY HIKING NOTES

TRAIL NAME

RATE/EXPERIENCE

DATE

LOCATION

COMPANIONS

WEATHER CONDITION

☐ ☐ ☐ ☐ ☐

TERRAIN LEVEL

easy ☐ ☐ ☐ ☐ ☐ hard

TRAIL TYPE

Out & back ☐ Loop ☐

One way ☐ Other ☐

MILESTONES

START TIME

END TIME

DURATION

DISTANCE

ALTITUDE

GEAR & EQUIPMENT

HIGHLIGHTS

TO DO NEXT TIME

MY HIKING NOTES

TRAIL NAME

RATE/EXPERIENCE

DATE

LOCATION

COMPANIONS

WEATHER CONDITION

START TIME

END TIME

DURATION

DISTANCE

ALTITUDE

TERRAIN LEVEL

easy ☐ ☐ ☐ ☐ ☐ hard

GEAR & EQUIPMENT

TRAIL TYPE

Out & back ☐ Loop ☐

One way ☐ Other ☐

MILESTONES

HIGHLIGHTS

TO DO NEXT TIME

MY HIKING NOTES

TRAIL NAME

RATE/EXPERIENCE

DATE

LOCATION

COMPANIONS

WEATHER CONDITION

START TIME

END TIME

DURATION

DISTANCE

ALTITUDE

TERRAIN LEVEL

easy hard

GEAR & EQUIPMENT

TRAIL TYPE

Out & back

Loop

One way

Other

MILESTONES

HIGHLIGHTS

TO DO NEXT TIME

MY HIKING NOTES

TRAIL NAME

RATE/EXPERIENCE

DATE

LOCATION

COMPANIONS

WEATHER CONDITION

☐ ☐ ☐ ☐ ☐

TERRAIN LEVEL

easy ☐ ☐ ☐ ☐ ☐ hard

TRAIL TYPE

Out & back ☐ Loop ☐

One way ☐ Other ☐

MILESTONES

START TIME

END TIME

DURATION

DISTANCE

ALTITUDE

GEAR & EQUIPMENT

HIGHLIGHTS

TO DO NEXT TIME

MY HIKING NOTES

TRAIL NAME

RATE/EXPERIENCE

DATE

LOCATION

COMPANIONS

WEATHER CONDITION

START TIME

END TIME

DURATION

DISTANCE

ALTITUDE

TERRAIN LEVEL

easy hard

GEAR & EQUIPMENT

TRAIL TYPE

Out & back

Loop

One way

Other

MILESTONES

HIGHLIGHTS

TO DO NEXT TIME

MY HIKING NOTES

TRAIL NAME

RATE/EXPERIENCE

DATE ____________

LOCATION ____________

COMPANIONS ____________

WEATHER CONDITION

☐ ☐ ☐ ☐ ☐

START TIME ____________

END TIME ____________

DURATION ____________

DISTANCE ____________

ALTITUDE ____________

TERRAIN LEVEL

easy ☐ ☐ ☐ ☐ ☐ hard

GEAR & EQUIPMENT

____

____

____

____

____

TRAIL TYPE

Out & back ☐ Loop ☐

One way ☐ Other ☐

MILESTONES

____

____

____

____

HIGHLIGHTS

____

____

____

____

TO DO NEXT TIME

____

____

MY HIKING NOTES

TRAIL NAME

RATE/EXPERIENCE

DATE

LOCATION

COMPANIONS

WEATHER CONDITION

TERRAIN LEVEL

easy ☐ ☐ ☐ ☐ ☐ hard

TRAIL TYPE

Out & back ☐ Loop ☐

One way ☐ Other ☐

START TIME

END TIME

DURATION

DISTANCE

ALTITUDE

GEAR & EQUIPMENT

MILESTONES

HIGHLIGHTS

TO DO NEXT TIME

MY HIKING NOTES

TRAIL NAME

RATE/EXPERIENCE

DATE

LOCATION

COMPANIONS

WEATHER CONDITION

START TIME

END TIME

DURATION

DISTANCE

ALTITUDE

TERRAIN LEVEL

easy hard

GEAR & EQUIPMENT

TRAIL TYPE

Out & back

Loop

One way

Other

MILESTONES

HIGHLIGHTS

TO DO NEXT TIME

MY HIKING NOTES

TRAIL NAME

RATE/EXPERIENCE

DATE

LOCATION

COMPANIONS

WEATHER CONDITION

START TIME

END TIME

DURATION

DISTANCE

ALTITUDE

TERRAIN LEVEL

easy ☐ ☐ ☐ ☐ ☐ hard

GEAR & EQUIPMENT

TRAIL TYPE

Out & back ☐ Loop ☐

One way ☐ Other ☐

MILESTONES

HIGHLIGHTS

TO DO NEXT TIME

MY HIKING NOTES

TRAIL NAME

RATE/EXPERIENCE

DATE

LOCATION

COMPANIONS

WEATHER CONDITION

START TIME

END TIME

DURATION

DISTANCE

ALTITUDE

TERRAIN LEVEL

easy ☐ ☐ ☐ ☐ ☐ hard

GEAR & EQUIPMENT

TRAIL TYPE

Out & back ☐ Loop ☐

One way ☐ Other ☐

MILESTONES

HIGHLIGHTS

TO DO NEXT TIME

MY HIKING NOTES

TRAIL NAME

RATE/EXPERIENCE

DATE

LOCATION

COMPANIONS

WEATHER CONDITION

TERRAIN LEVEL

easy ☐ ☐ ☐ ☐ ☐ hard

TRAIL TYPE

Out & back ☐ Loop ☐

One way ☐ Other ☐

START TIME

END TIME

DURATION

DISTANCE

ALTITUDE

GEAR & EQUIPMENT

MILESTONES

HIGHLIGHTS

TO DO NEXT TIME

MY HIKING NOTES

TRAIL NAME

RATE/EXPERIENCE

DATE

LOCATION

COMPANIONS

WEATHER CONDITION

TERRAIN LEVEL

easy ☐ ☐ ☐ ☐ ☐ hard

TRAIL TYPE

Out & back ☐ Loop ☐

One way ☐ Other ☐

MILESTONES

START TIME

END TIME

DURATION

DISTANCE

ALTITUDE

GEAR & EQUIPMENT

HIGHLIGHTS

TO DO NEXT TIME

MY HIKING NOTES

TRAIL NAME

RATE/EXPERIENCE

DATE

LOCATION

COMPANIONS

WEATHER CONDITION

START TIME

END TIME

DURATION

DISTANCE

ALTITUDE

TERRAIN LEVEL

easy ☐ ☐ ☐ ☐ ☐ hard

GEAR & EQUIPMENT

TRAIL TYPE

Out & back ☐ Loop ☐

One way ☐ Other ☐

MILESTONES

HIGHLIGHTS

TO DO NEXT TIME

MY HIKING NOTES

TRAIL NAME

RATE/EXPERIENCE

DATE

LOCATION

COMPANIONS

WEATHER CONDITION

TERRAIN LEVEL

easy □ □ □ □ □ hard

TRAIL TYPE

Out & back □ Loop □

One way □ Other □

MILESTONES

START TIME

END TIME

DURATION

DISTANCE

ALTITUDE

GEAR & EQUIPMENT

HIGHLIGHTS

TO DO NEXT TIME

MY HIKING NOTES

TRAIL NAME

RATE/EXPERIENCE

DATE

LOCATION

COMPANIONS

WEATHER CONDITION

TERRAIN LEVEL

easy hard

TRAIL TYPE

Out & back

Loop

One way

Other

START TIME

END TIME

DURATION

DISTANCE

ALTITUDE

GEAR & EQUIPMENT

MILESTONES

HIGHLIGHTS

TO DO NEXT TIME

MY HIKING NOTES

TRAIL NAME

RATE/EXPERIENCE

DATE

LOCATION

COMPANIONS

WEATHER CONDITION

START TIME

END TIME

DURATION

DISTANCE

ALTITUDE

TERRAIN LEVEL

easy ☐ ☐ ☐ ☐ ☐ hard

GEAR & EQUIPMENT

TRAIL TYPE

Out & back ☐ Loop ☐

One way ☐ Other ☐

MILESTONES

HIGHLIGHTS

TO DO NEXT TIME

MY HIKING NOTES

YOUR OPINION MATTERS TO ME!

PLEASE LET ME KNOW HOW YOU FEEL ABOUT THE HIKING JOURNAL AT:

MOONTTI.BOOKS@GMAIL.COM

Printed in Dunstable, United Kingdom